# From Within

Nguénar Yacine Cissé

ISBN-13: 978-1-0697924-0-2

Cover art and illustrations by Nahida Diaba

# Acknowledgements

Many thanks to all who have contributed to the creative process that led to the publishing of this work. To name each would risk omission, so I simply acknowledge, recognize, and thank every single person who has engaged with this work through their contribution, support, feedback, critique, and encouragement in countless ways.

To my family — thank you for accepting me as I am and for continuing, each day, to be my reason to do good and to keep going.

Above all, praise and thanks to God, who has granted me the courage, awareness of my abilities, and the life to bring this work into being.

# Author's Note

*From Within* is a journey into the heart—the place where all emotions, experiences, and beliefs are born and shaped.

In this collection, I explore the complex layers of life—emotion, love, and the quiet yet profound strength that comes from faith. From the vivid hues of life's joy and sorrow, to the depth of love's vulnerability, to the grounding peace of spiritual surrender, this book is my attempt to capture what lies *from within*. I have always believed that the answers we seek often exist within us, waiting to be uncovered in the quiet moments of reflection.

Rooted in the culture of my Senegalese heritage and the wisdom passed down through generations, *From Within* is also a tribute to the rich tradition of storytelling. The quiet strength of the baobab tree and the soft embrace of *teranga* (hospitality) have shaped not only this collection but the way I move through the world. My faith in Islam and the concept of *tawakkul*—trusting in God's will and surrendering to the divine plan—has been the foundation of my spiritual journey, and I've woven these themes into my poetry as a way to honor both my personal and communal identity.

These poems speak to the universal human experience—of longing, of loss, of hope, and of finding peace in the midst of chaos. I hope that, through these words, you too may find something that resonates with your own journey from within.

Thank you for taking this journey with me.

With care,

Nguénar Yacine Cissé

# Table of Contents

# Emotional Palette

## MEMORIES

There is always a sadness in memories.
Maybe it's because,
Like the people you lost,
They are only the fleeting seconds
Your mind allows you to hold onto—
Until reality intrudes,
And reminds you they are gone.
Just like that,
Your eyes blur.

## GONE

My bones—
Fragile in comparison
To the cold concrete beneath,
With which they were acquainted.
In a matter of seconds,
I fell.
My hopes scattered,
Like beads from my bracelet,
Each one hitting hard—
A moment lost.

## TRACES

The past has a familiar smell—
Like an old room,
Or a breath of wind from years ago.
But not all memories
Are alike in odor.
Some cling like smoke,
Others pass like perfume.
Some we chase.
Some we wish would fade.

## MIRROR TALK

It's a different kind of shame
When I couldn't meet my own eyes
In the mirror—
Not because I feared the truth,
But because I had none
To soothe myself with.

I broke down,
But not in a way the world could see.
It was internal—
A quiet kind of collapse
That sat heavy on my chest,
Made heavier by the weight
Of the decisions I made
That are now hurting.

Maybe shame
Is the wrong description
For the ache of being unable
To go back in time—
To undo,
To unchoose,
To reimagine a version of me
That didn't fall this way.

## ENCODED

In this moment that time stood still,
I wished how I felt
Could be transcribed
Onto a storage card,
Translated into byte sizes—
A language for any software to read.
So maybe then,
You'd understand
The inexplicable way I feel,
Without my need
To speak.

## SWEET TOUCH SOUR FEEL

Virgin waters he sailed through
Paddling and working diligently,
Or shall I say strategically?

The waters pure, innocent,
Carrying a slight treble,
Mesmerizing.

As the sailor entered the canal,
She began agonizing,
In a way that words could not express.
Understandable,
She craved his presence while he was present.

He is not the first, nor will he be the last,
To roam these waters with no intention
To abide therein forever.
The waters had believed and hoped,
With each passage,
That the sailor would stay.

## CONSCIENCE

Hope has deceived me—
In a mysterious affair.
It hauled clouds of thought
Into my mind
And hummed quiet feelings
Into my heart.

I sought the culprit
Behind this elaborate scheme,
Only to find—
None other than
My imagination.

# TIME MACHINE

What is time,
When I reminisce
About my past
In the stillness of
The present moment?

What is time,
When I let my then
Disrupt my now?

What is time,
When the past steals me—
Even if only for a moment—
While I dream of the future?

What is time,
When I wish this past
Would settle,
So I could live for now—
And for what's to come?

## LULLABY

Sometimes silence is deafening,
In its screeching, relentless drag—
So much so, I want nothing to do with it.

Other times, silence is the right amount
Of space I need,
For the nothingness around me
To embrace me,
And lull me into calming states.

## AGAIN

To walk through days
And feel the ground pull you nowhere.

To cradle hurt in both arms,
Heavy as stone,
Yet be numb to its weight.

To drift like a ghost
In a world of breathing bodies.

To harbor a roar—
Locked behind the gate of your throat.

And still,
To hold in your chest
The quiet miracle
Of being reborn
Before you leave.

## EUPHORIA

Unicorns, rainbows, and colors it is not.
My happy place is in a corner,
Where I cannot be called or reached.
Sometimes it is a place of sadness,
Sometimes a space I feel at ease,
Sometimes, it just is.
My happy place is distant—
A quiet space
Where I aim to be at peace with myself.

## ALIVE

In the stillness of being,
I found the rhythm of living—
For you, as you are.

The world seeks a manual to see you;
You are its author.

## POTENTIAL

"Maybe one day"
Is not a flag
I get to fly high
In abandonment
Of my dreams.

"Maybe one day"
Is not a white flag
I raise in surrender
Of my promises.

"Maybe one day"
Is not a banner
I wave in arrest
Of the great things
I can do—
Starting now.

## DESTINY

Where I have been
Reminds me of places
I never want to return to.
Destinations that once held me,
But no longer define me.

Where I have been
Holds hope for where I could go—
A calling carried in the wind
Toward gentler, wider spaces.

Where journeys bump shoulders,
Eager to sing their stories
Of paths crossed and detours taken,
Of lessons earned.

When the wind howls,
Where I've been
And where I could be
Meet me where I am now—
Whispering secrets about me
That I will only come to know
When I arrive
At the place I was always meant to be.

# Hues of Life

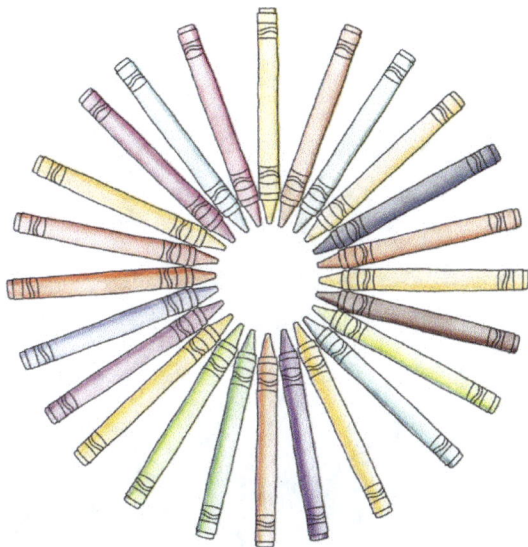

## ACQUAINTANCE

We almost never remember
How we met people.
How they left,
That is what remains—
Engraved in us.

## SOCIETY

There were days when
She was empty,
And he lost.
There were days when
They were abandoned,
And we were scarred
By irreversible actions.

## SOCIAL CIRCLE

There you are,
Clinging to what never existed,
Falling for the illusion of attention,
After a string of deceit.
Silence, now, is the only proof
Of a lesson learned.

## CYCLE

I watched as events passed by,
A movie tape rolling before my eyes.
Silence filled the space
Where I could have said, "I told you so."

## WHEN NIGHT FALLS

The ghost of a past you've healed from is sneaky—
It lures you to claim you've moved on,
Only to prove you haven't.
It slips into the narrow canals of the mind,
Creeping in when night falls,
Unseen, impossible to hide away.

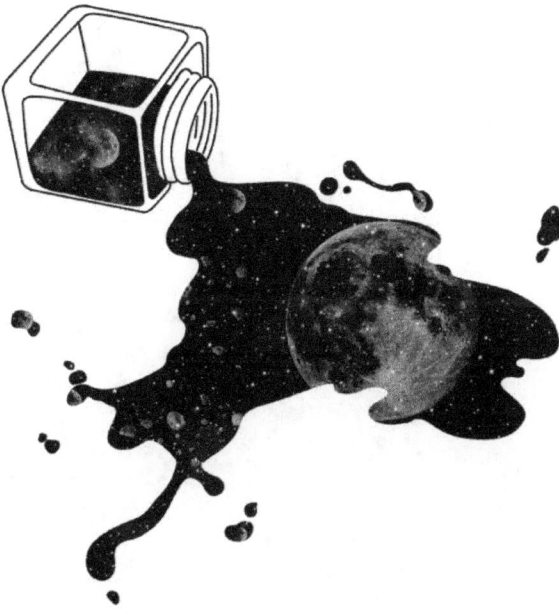

## GOSSIP CHAIN

Trust and loyalty—meant to be a two-way system.
But truly,
Are those on the receiving end true to each other?
Or are there more players in this loyalty
Than the other ever knows?

## HUES OF LIFE

Life in colors would be pink—
A hue of baby pink,
To symbolize
The sweet nothings that
Coat harsh realities,
Shaping the edges.

Relationships would be blue,
Royal blue, or ocean blue,
To reflect the depth of
Experiences they bring.

Part of me clings
To the imagery
Of ocean-blue.
What a valid scene!
For you and I couldn't keep
Our heads above water—
So we drowned along with
Our love, and the hopes
It birthed.

## WHAT FOLLOWS

We fear endings,
The discomfort we feel when things are no longer.
Is it the emptiness that follows we despise,
Or the feeling of having nothing left?

## In Passing

I was in the water—
The salt from Saly Portudal's
Waves stung my cheeks,
After the air and breeze
Kissed me hello.

I was in the water,
In Port Dickson,
Where the instant switch
From warm to cool
Tingled—softly,
As the tides rushed
To and fro,
Carrying secrets.

I was in the water,
In Lake Geneva,
Subtly battling the cold,
As we had missed each other.

If water carries memory,
At the meeting of rivers and oceans,
Do the waters recall
My presence—
And long for me still?
It's been years,
I wonder.

# JOURNEY

To have self-love
Is not a constant—
It's not a steady-state.
It's an eternal battle,
Or an eternal journey—
Make it as you wish.
But there is beauty in it all.

## WEIGHT OF ME

You couldn't bear the weight of me—
The gravity of my essence,
The dense force I carried,
The tremors I sent rippling through your life.

You couldn't handle me.
But "couldn't handle" feels too simple,
Too soft, too light, too gentle
For how you truly shattered
The space we shared—
Because you couldn't stand steady enough
To meet what I was.

## THE HIGHWAY

Life is meant for living—
Not through you.
Life is meant for living—
Not through your fears.
Life is meant for living—
Not through your trauma.
Life is meant for living—
Not through your experiences.

Life is meant for living—
By making my own choices,
By trusting my own decisions,
By making my own mistakes.
Life is meant for living—
Not through anybody else.

## SUNSHINE

Life gave me rain,
So I let flowers bloom.

In the thunder's roar
And silvered showers,
I cleansed myself.

When the sun's rays
Were too shy to break the clouds,
I closed my eyes
And found their warmth
Within.

# HOMESICK

Let me tell you about the land
I am from.
One where the sand—
Darkish, brownish, reddish—
As if it were trying to mimic
The color of my skin,
Ish.

Let me tell you about Senegal,
**Suñu Gaal**,
Our boat, where we rock with the **Baye Fall**,
Where we stand arm in arm,
In the spirit of **Teranga**.

Let me tell you about **Dakar**,
Where my New York-born brother
Fell in love with
**Tangana**.
No, she is not a girl,
But I'd bet he'd still call her sweet.

Let me tell you about a place of rhythm,
Where to the beat of the drums
Women dance **sabar**,
A beat that rings in my ears,
Even an ocean away,
As I am still with them...
As a child of the land of **Teranga**.

# The Love Scheme

## YOUTH

I was promised forever,
But it took me time to see—
Forever is no longer an eternity.
It is no longer an open-ended vow,
Nor a time frame of unconditional love.

## HEART BROKEN

You broke something—
Something of mine
You knew was plastic.
Not fake—
But plastic:
It could take back its shape.
It could.
"Could"—
Nothing but a possibility.

## COMPANY

Love,
A guest unannounced—
Always.

I opened my doors
Wholeheartedly.
Had I known it would
Shatter the place,
I wouldn't have asked it
To stay longer.

Nguénar Yacine Cissé

## STORYLINE

I cried for you a river
You never wanted to swim in.
I drifted on clouds for you—
Daydreaming,
Leaving reality behind.

I thought I could teach you
The steps to this dance,
But maybe I wrote a storyline
Laced with flaws,
Starting with calling you
My person.

## CRICKETS...

You gave me silence.
In the echo, I found
A space—
A rhythm too familiar.

You gave me silence.
Time opened its arms
So I could decide who you were.

You gave me silence.
A blank page,
My mind filled in for you.
And now,
That silence speaks louder
Than anything you ever said.

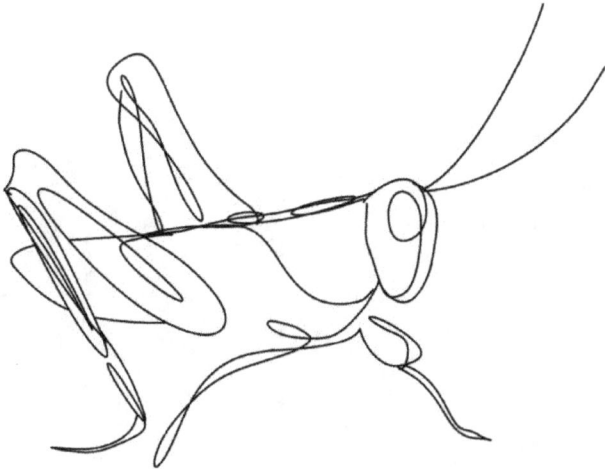

## OASIS

You found my vessel with substance—
Not full,
But never empty.

To think you've left me deserted
Is blasphemy.

## FROM THE HEART

Love is a paradox.
Selfish, yet selfless.
You give pieces of yourself
For someone else to feel,
And in return,
You hope for reciprocity—
An exchange of pieces,
Of presence,
Of one another.

But what if the experience
Strips you instead?
You expect selfless love,
In return for your
Selfish offering.

You walk full, yet half-empty.
Because the love you gave
Cost you more
Than you could bear.

Such is the price of love—
Knowing you may never
Leave the experience whole.

Is it selfish of me
To love selfishly
When I no longer have
Selfless love in me?

# FROM THE HEART (CONT.)

Is it selfish of me
To miss
The version of myself
Capable of selfless love,
But too tired to conjure her?

Is it selfish of me
To deprive myself
Of the beauty
That a selfless love can birth?
One where both parties
Go at it full force,
And unconditionally?

Yet, a soft crash is better
Than a hard crash.

So I wonder,
Can you dose love?
Will love allow itself
To be conditioned?
Or is love wild and raw
In how it presents?

## CONFESSION

I miss you,
I must admit.

I am bankrupt,
I must admit,
Of emotional currency
To pour into
This journey
Of entanglement.

But I miss you,
And I must admit.

## ENGRAVED

I groomed my heart to tolerate you—
So much so that no one else fits
Its intricate crevices like you do.

Maybe it had nothing to do
With me, but everything to do
With who you are.

Perhaps the imprint you left
Ran too deep,
Engraving truths
I didn't know existed.

## Before Dawn

Sometimes, there is no reason—
My heart ran to you,
Not knowing why.

Even in loss,
You are enough.

At night,
Memories light the flame again.

But love is not everything,
So before dawn,
I let you go.

## To Love

Is it a necessity or a commodity?
Will I be alright with none but
My own weight to carry by my side?

To love—
Is it a commodity that some get to enjoy
While others cannot afford its hypnotizing
Enchant?

What is love when the cool morning winter breeze
And my favorite tune make it a necessity?
Whilst the lack of finding my flavor
Makes it a commodity?

## SELF-LOVE

Be there for me,
As you have always been—
Most gracious,
Most precious—
Stay.

Ease my soul, so heavy.
Dare to have self-love,
Dare to love me.

Stay strong,
Stay real,
Be true.
Dare to have self-love,
Dare to love me.

## LOVE FOR YOU

Don't think you're unlovable
Just because you sought
Love
Where it wasn't ready
To hold you.

## HONEY

I am a hopeless romantic—
Maybe.
But I like to think
There's nothing hopeless about
Romance.

It is full of hope,
Full of new days,
Full of chances.

Romance is what you make it,
And mine is full of hope.
Love pours in by the minute—
Like bees at work in the heart
Of a honeycomb,
Providing something sweet.

## NIKKAH

I am rightfully yours.
You don't need a map
To explore this terrain.
You have my permission
To conquer and establish
Every birthmark you find
As your territory.

# In Faith

## Infinite

Misery in infinity is not my destiny.
This journey may seem prolonged,
But fortunately for me,
I am the servant of a Deity
Who faces no constraint,
To whom I can call endlessly.
He is always there,
In infinity.

Nguénar Yacine Cissé

# Rūh

When my soul regains its natural state,
From my eyes flows the Kawthar—
A river of abundance.
From it flows my sins,
From it flows sorrow and despair,
But from it flows hope in my case.

As I call out to Al-Wakeel,
The Disposer of Affairs,
My soul feels secure in its vulnerability.
It regains its natural state of worship—
A state it has always known.

From the beginning of time,
My Rūh has been placed in me
To worship Rabbul Alamin.
But at times,
I lose focus.

## PUSH AND PULL

When the heart and mind
Enter a game of tug-of-war,
Both pulling with equal force,
How does one mediate
Between the two?

When the science of logic
No longer feels logical,
Or the pull of the heart
Is more firm,
Restricting the mind from reason,
I wish nothing but to
Entrust my affairs
To the Trustee of Affairs.

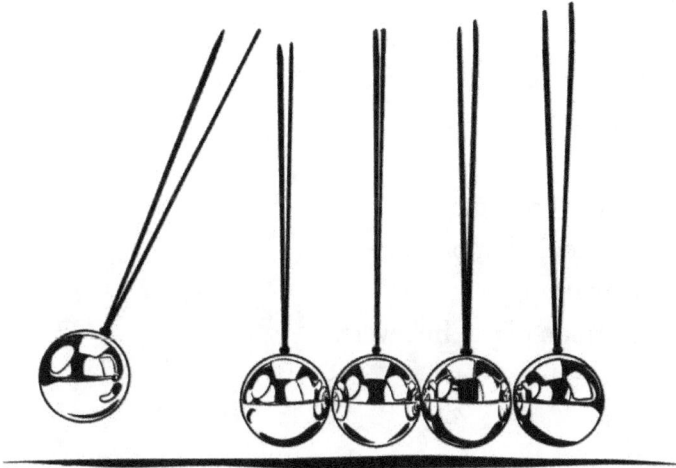

## 2:257

The weight of
What is and what isn't
Sits heavy on my heart,
Compressing everything within,
Pressed against my chest.

As the pressure builds,
The only places I feel—
My chest, throat, and eyes—
Burn too,
In comradeship.

When I catch a moment
In a breath,
"Alhamdoulilah"
Escapes effortlessly,
For what has passed
And what is to come.

In the tang of despair,
There suddenly is a pleasure
In remembering
The Guardian of the Believers.

## TYPE

My kind of love
Is like the sun kissing
The mountain tops with warmth,
A little after dawn...
Patient and consistent.

My kind of love
Is like the clear seas...
Transparent.

My kind of love
Is like a mother's love
For her child—
But a little more than that.
It is like Allah's love
For His creation...
Rahim.

## DIVINE

Kun Faya Kun,
"Be, and it is."
Allah said "Be,"
And it was.

You are the product of
Kun Faya Kun,
So how could I ever look at you
With eyes other than
Those of love?

## FOREVER

I asked my Rabb for forever with you,
Not once considering the possibility
Of forever meaning "in the next life."
Maybe there is more romance in being
A lover of the Akhirah.

## EMBRACE

Maybe one day,
You won't have to wake up
And wonder.
I will no longer be someone
From your imagination.
I will be there
When you look back,
Ready to take you
As you are,
Ready to give you
All I have,
Ready to finally embrace
Who the Best of Planners
Has written for me.

## DIVINE WORLD

My name next to yours,
In the divine world.
You and I were chosen,
In the divine world.
I can't wait to meet you,
Here and there,
In the divine world.

## SUSTENANCE

Like clouds yielding to the wind,
I drift through the shifting shades of sky—
Tawakkul.
I move with the day's quiet current,
Trusting what is mine will find me,
And that the One who guides the clouds
Will place in my hands
All I need to overcome.

## THE BIRDS

Like the birds You hold up in the sky,
I want to rely on You—unconditionally.
To know I will catch a worm—
But leave the when and where to You.

To know hunger may visit me,
But that You will feed me to fullness.
Like the birds, I will go out each day,
Carrying nothing—yet lacking nothing.

For my nothing, and my everything,
Rests with You.

## AL MUJEEB (THE ONE WHO RESPONDS)

In sickness and in health,
In hope and in despair,
In clarity and in burden—
When I have no one, I have Him.

No matter how far I wander,
He is near—closer than my jugular vein.
A closeness I cannot grasp,
Yet I take comfort in it.

In darkness and light,
In noise and silence,
In presence and absence—
He is always there.

He was there when I forgot,
There when I returned,
There when no one else remained.

In sickness and in health—
When there is no one,
There is always Him.

## The Most Loving

**To Be Loved**
Al-Wadud has loved me enough
To give me a chance.

**To Be the Prize**
He has chosen me
To be among His creation.

**To Be Given the Chance**
He has blessed me
With the ability to worship Him.

**To Have the Choice**
In good and in bad,
I remember Him.

**To Choose My Battle**
One path is heavy,
The other just as steep—
Still, I choose His way.

And so I walk,
Loved, chosen, guided—
Toward Him.

## WITH YOU

What I thought impossible,
You proved within reach—
For You hold no limitation.

When I believed
I had passed the point of return,
You revealed to me
That life holds more than one journey.

Each journey carries its own theme.
Each chapter, a soul in test.
Each trial,
An invitation to come closer to You.

And every step—
Even the weary ones—
Is made worthwhile
With You in heart,
In mind,
In motion.

The hymn of this life
Is only bearable
With You by my side.

# About the Author

Nguénar Yacine is a poet and development practitioner whose work weaves themes of life, love, faith, and self-discovery. Beginning to write poetry at fifteen, Yacine embraced it as a form of expression and reflection, later compiling years of journaling into a collection that speaks to both vulnerability and hope. Her debut poetry book captures moments born from lived experience, epiphanies, and imagination, inviting readers to pause, reflect, and connect with the hues of life in all their forms.